Control Order 351

Antoinette Moses

Series Editors:
Rob Waring and Sue Leather

Series Story Consultant: Julian Thomlinson

NATIONAL
GEOGRAPHIC
LEARNING | CENGAGE
Learning·

Australia • Brazil • Japan • Korea • Mexico • Singapore • Spain • United Kingdom • United States

Page Turners Reading Library
Control Order 351
Antoinette Moses

Publisher: Andrew Robinson

Executive Editor: Sean Bermingham

Associate Development Editor:
Sarah Tan

Editorial Assistant: Vivian Chua

Director of Global Marketing:
Ian Martin

Senior Content Project Manager:
Tan Jin Hock

Manufacturing Planner:
Mary Beth Hennebury

Contributor: Jessie Chew

Layout Design and Illustrations:
Redbean Design Pte Ltd

Cover Illustration: Eric Foenander

Photo Credits:
88 RedDaxLuma/Shutterstock

ISBN-13: 978-1-4240-4889-2

ISBN-10: 1-4240-4889-3

National Geographic Learning
20 Channel Center Street
Boston, Massachusetts 02210
USA

Cengage Learning is a leading provider of
customized learning solutions with office
locations around the globe, including
Singapore, the United Kingdom, Australia,
Mexico, Brazil, and Japan. Locate your local
office at:
international.cengage.com/region

Cengage Learning products are represented
in Canada by Nelson Education, Ltd.

Visit National Geographic Learning online at
NGL.Cengage.com

Visit our corporate website at
www.cengage.com

Printed in the United States of America
1 2 3 4 5 6 7 – 17 16 15 14 13

Contents

Review

Background Reading

People in the story

Alex Davidson
a boy in his late teens, who lives
with his mother and sister in
Central London

Steve Burke
Alex's friend

Suze Stephens
Alex's girlfriend

Vic Hall
a policeman

Matt
a policeman

Solo
an "Outsider," who lives
outside Central London

The story is set in London and other parts of Great Britain
in the year 2110.

Prologue

The year is 2110.

The world is still recovering from a long global war over natural resources. With food, water, oil, minerals, and other necessities now in short supply, countries are saving their scarce resources for themselves. Every country is on its own.

In this climate of suspicion and fear, a totalitarian government has come to power in Britain. For twenty years now, this government has restricted the freedom of British citizens in the name of national security.

But perhaps not for much longer . . .

Chapter 1

A new order

20.8.2110. 17.30.

The kitchen was full of noise. Pink cats danced in a green garden and sang a song about saving water. "We save water every day. What about you?" sang the cats. A teenage girl and her older brother were singing along with the cats and laughing. Their mother sighed as she looked up from the list she was writing.

"Alex!" his mother said crossly. "Alex, are you listening to me?"

"What?" replied her son.

"Turn that thing off!" Mrs. Davidson told her daughter.

"But I'm watching it, Mom," said Tish.

"I read that in the twenty-first century they had hundreds of TV channels," said Alex. "Now we've only got the news channel and the public service channel. It's so boring."

"Hundreds!" said Tish. "That's amazing. It's not true, is it, Mom?"

"I don't know," said Mrs. Davidson. "Whatever else you may think, I was not alive a hundred years ago."

"I know," said Tish, "but didn't you learn about it at school?"

"When I was young," said her mother, "there wasn't a nice school like the one you go to. The war was still on, remember?"

"Yeah, we remember," Alex sighed and rolled his eyes. "You never stop telling us about it."

"Dad never talks much about the war, Mom," said Tish. "Why?"

"Your father doesn't like to keep talking about the bad things that happened in the past," said Mrs. Davidson. "He tries to make a better world. That's why he's a doctor."

"He never talks much about anything," said Alex.

"That's because you two never stop talking long enough to give him a chance," laughed their mother. "But I'm trying to write a list," she continued. "Now, Alex, please think about your birthday."

"OK," Alex said as he stretched lazily. "I wasn't really watching TV. But I want to phone Suze first." He picked up the phone. "I've been ringing her all evening and she doesn't answer."

"Suze is probably busy," said Mrs. Davidson. "Anyhow," she continued, "you can talk to your girlfriend later. I'm trying to organize your birthday party. You wanted a big party, so you'd better help me plan it!"

"Did you see Suze today?" Alex asked Tish.

"No," said Tish. "But I don't see her every day. We're not in all of the same classes. Suze is an A Plus."

Tish and Suze were both sixteen and in the same year at school.

"Suze is an A Plus because she works hard," said Mrs. Davidson.

"I work hard," said Tish.

"Yes," said Alex, making fun of his sister. "You work

hard at the things you like. Like drama and art."

"There's nothing wrong with that," said Tish. "Just because you like history!"

"Will you both stop arguing!" said Mrs. Davidson. "I still have plenty of things to do this evening, and I need to send the guest list for Alex's birthday party to the Control Room."

"Why?" asked Tish.

"Because it's going to be a big party." Mrs. Davidson picked up her pen. "You know the law, Tish. According to Control Order 273, if we have any group activity with more than 30 people, we have to send all the names a week before the event to the Control Room. It's not new."

"Oh yes," said Tish. "It's just that there are so many Control Orders, it's hard sometimes to remember them all."

"I know it seems difficult, Tish. But following the rules makes life safer for all of us," her mother responded. "Anyway, go upstairs and do your homework now. Your father will soon be home and it will be time for dinner."

Home for the Davidsons was a large old house in a circle of houses in Central London. Mrs. Davidson knew her family was lucky to have this house. So many houses had gone in the war. And this house was old. The main building was probably hundreds of years old, and the garden was big enough for two large wind turbines to produce all the energy they needed. They also had space to grow vegetables and fruit, and to keep chickens and rabbits. Very few people in London were so fortunate, but Mrs. Davidson doubted that her children realized just how lucky they were.

"Put down the phone, Alex," said Mrs. Davidson. "Tish!

Are you still . . ." She was interrupted by the sound of the telephone ringing.

"See, it's ringing anyway," said Alex. "Hello?" He said into the phone. "Oh, Mrs. Stephens, I thought you were Suze. What? OK . . .

"It's Suze's mom," he said to his mother, surprised. "She wants to talk to you."

Mrs. Davidson took the phone. "Hello, Lucy," she said. "What's the matter? What's happened?" She turned to her son. "Put on the news channel," Mrs. Davidson told him urgently.

Alex changed the TV channels. The face of a reporter appeared on the screen.

"I'm here in New Downing Street," said the reporter. "We are waiting for the Prime Minister. Here he comes now." The Prime Minister stepped in front of the microphones.

"I am going to make a short statement," said the Prime Minister. "This country is in danger. We have worked hard for many years to make sure that there is enough food and water for every person in Britain. But the population continues to grow. Today's decision has not been an easy one. But we have to do something because I have to make sure that all of you have enough food and water. That is why today your government has created a new Control Order. This is Control Order 351. There is not enough food for everyone and we have to put the British first. We are therefore sending all foreigners home. All foreigners, and those whose parents are foreign, must go to the nearest police station."

The Prime Minister smiled at the cameras. "We live in difficult times. During the long war, this great country was in terrible

danger. Even now we all have to work hard for everything that we have. Your government has to do what is best for Britain. We have prepared special detention camps where all foreigners can live until they are put on ships and returned to their country of origin. As of today, all those who have one parent who wasn't born in Britain will be considered foreign. We must make Britain safe for the British. Thank you."

Mrs. Davidson listened to the Prime Minister and then picked up the phone again.

"Yes, Lucy, I heard the Prime Minister," she said. "But you're not a foreigner. What are you afraid of?"

"What is it, Mom?" asked Alex.

"I'm so sorry," said Mrs. Davidson into the phone. "Lucy, I didn't know."

"You didn't know what?" asked Tish.

Mrs. Davidson put down the phone. Her children moved toward her. They knew something bad had happened.

"Is it about Suze?" asked Tish.

"Where is she? I must go and talk with her," said Alex. He was already moving toward the door.

"Sit down, Alex," his mother told him. "Yes, it is about Suze. I don't know whether you know this, but Suze is an adopted child. She was adopted by Lucy and her husband. Suze's own parents died when she was just a baby. But they were not British, they came from Canada. The government now considers Suze a foreigner."

Mrs. Davidson's voice softened as she looked into her son's horror-filled eyes. "I'm so sorry, Alex. Suze was picked up by the police this morning. They've taken her away to a detention camp."

Chapter 2

A new life

20.8.2110. 17.40.

"I think that's everything," said Mrs. Hall. She wrapped a large plate and put it into a box. She turned to her husband. "Isn't it wonderful? We're going to live in the Police Village. We'll be free of all this."

Mrs. Hall waved her arm toward the windows. Her husband, Jack, looked out. From the third-floor windows of their flat they could see most of the North London district. He looked down at the houses in rows below; they looked like lines of soldiers who had lost the war. Some of the houses had fallen down and most of them were black from the smoke of many fires.

Every night there were fires in the streets. But nobody ever came to put out the flames. Nobody entered North London at night. At night the streets belonged to the Outsiders—the men and women with guns. But recently the Outsiders had begun to wander around the streets during the day. The police and the army were always trying to get rid of the Outsiders, but they never seemed to succeed. Mrs. Hall wondered where they came from. Outsiders were outside society; they could not go to shops or to hospitals. She did not know how they survived.

As Mrs. Hall watched the street, there came the sound of a gun somewhere in the neighborhood. North London was a place of fire and guns.

"We won't be sorry to leave here, will we, Jack?" Mrs. Hall asked her husband.

"No, we won't be sorry to leave," he agreed. "Just think, Patti, the Police Village! It's going to be a new life for us."

"It's thanks to you, Vic." Mrs. Hall turned to the young man sitting on a chair in the corner, frowning as he talked on the phone.

"What?" asked Vic. "Yes," he spoke into the phone. "I'll put the television on now and I'll see you tomorrow."

"You should stop chatting on the phone when your mother is speaking to you," said Jack.

Vic put down the phone. "Sorry, Dad. It's the Police Center. There are things I need to speak with them about. It's important."

"Of course it is," said his mother, smiling. "You're going to be a policeman."

"And," she added, "you're going to be eighteen. We could have a party in our new flat."

"No, Mom," said Vic. "No party. A policeman doesn't have time for parties. It's a serious job. And now there's this new Control Order, I'll be working day and night."

He moved across the room to the television and turned it on.

"What new Control Order?" asked his father.

"They've just announced it," he said. "There's something on tonight's news. We need to see it." Vic turned on the television news, and he and his parents watched the Prime Minister's statement.

Vic's father cheered when the Prime Minister finished. "Wonderful! This is exactly what the country needs. We've waited a long time for Control Order 351. I've been saying this for years, haven't I, Patti?"

"Yes, Jack," agreed his wife. "You always say that there are too many newcomers."

"Well, there are. My family has lived in Britain for centuries, but I bet half the people in this city have come here in the last twenty years. What right do they have to live off our country?"

"Yes, Jack," said his wife, nodding. She turned to her son.

"You're doing a very important job, Vic," she said. "Your father and I are very proud of you."

Vic's face went red. "Yeah," he said. "Thanks, Mom."

Vic was never much good at talking, and he was particularly bad at talking about himself, but he felt that today was one of the happiest days of his life. He could see how thrilled his parents were and he knew that he was responsible for their happiness. He, too, had waited for this day for a long time.

The North London district was poor and dangerous. It had always been poor and dangerous. Every day of his childhood he had come home afraid. Every day he turned the corner of the street and looked for his house. Was it still there? Had there been a fire? Were his parents still alive? He'd always felt that it was his job to make sure that his parents were safe. He had first thought that when he was six years old and he still felt it today. And now, finally, they were going to be safe. They were going to live in the Police Village, the safest district in London. And he had made it possible.

Vic had worked and worked to become a policeman. It had not been easy. All the best schools were for people with money. You had to pay for education and his parents never had enough money to buy him a place at a good school. So he'd gotten a job as a classroom guard at a private school. Vic watched and listened and learned. He watched the rich boys and knew that he was not like them. Everything for them was so easy. Too easy.

Their laughter was too easy, their smiles were too easy. They knew nothing of the world outside. Vic hated them, but he smiled at them when he saw them and he never told anybody his feelings.

When he was fourteen, he won a place at a government school. The best students at the school became police officers or soldiers. There were hard exams every year and if you did not pass them, you left the school. There were no second chances. You passed or you were out. Vic passed every year; he was one of the best students in the school.

And now he was going to be the best policeman in London. His parents were going to be even more proud of him.

Chapter 3

"I have to rescue Suze."

20.8.2110. 17.45.

Tish began to cry. Tears streamed down her face and she didn't even try to wipe them away.

"Suze is in a camp?" asked Alex. "She doesn't belong in a camp! How can they take her away just like that? We have to do something."

"What?" wept Tish. "What can we do?"

"I don't know! Something!" shouted Alex. He got up and stormed to the door.

"You're not going out," said Mrs. Davidson. "You don't have a movement order." She picked up the phone. "I have to tell your father."

"Don't you understand, Mom? I can't just sit here when Suze is in a camp!" Alex was furious. "I've got to do *something*!"

"Don't shout at me," said his mother. "I know it's hard, but there's nothing you can do. It's the law!"

"I hate Control Orders," said Tish. "You can't meet your friends or go out after nine o'clock. You can't have a party without sending the Control Room a list. It says in the history books that you used to be able to do anything."

"Yes, and what happened?" asked her mother. "There was violence and war, and people fought in the streets."

"There's still lots of violence and fighting in London," said Alex.

"Yes," replied his mother, "but it's not here. We don't have it in our area. The world was a very dangerous place a hundred years ago."

"I think people still do the same things," said Alex. "And Steve's father thinks that the old world was better."

"Steve's father thinks a lot of things," said his mother quickly. "You know that he lost his job at the newspaper because of things he said. I don't want you listening to that kind of talk. Talk like that doesn't help anyone."

"Steve's my best friend," said Alex. "And I like Mr. Burke."

"I like Steve, too," sighed his mother. "And I like the Burkes. But it's dangerous to say these things. I worry."

"Yes," her son burst out angrily. "Because if you criticize the government, you may end up in a camp!" He stood up. "Maybe I should speak out and then they'll send me to the same camp as Suze."

"Don't be stupid," said his mother. "You don't even know where Suze is."

"No," said Alex. *But I'm going to find out*, he promised himself. He looked at the clock on the wall. Like many things in the Davidson home, it was old and beautiful. *Maybe things really were better in the past*, thought Alex. *I hate this world.* He felt like he'd been living in a safe, comfortable bubble. And it had just burst.

"I'm going to Steve's," he told his mother. "Don't worry, Mom," he added as he kissed her. "I won't do anything stupid."

"Of course I worry," called his mother after him. "That's what mothers do!"

◇◇◇

The Burkes lived in a smaller house in the same neighborhood. It had a flat roof with several solar panels to catch the energy of the sun, and small wind machines. Steve and his parents were having tea when Alex arrived.

"Have you heard about the new Control Order?" asked Steve. Alex nodded and told his friend about Suze.

"That's terrible," cried Steve. "Do you know where she is?" he asked Alex, before turning to his father. "Dad," he continued, without waiting for Alex to reply, "Do you know where the camps are?" The two boys had been friends for so many years that they often knew what the other was thinking.

His father hesitated. "No, I don't."

"But you know people who will know," insisted his son.

"Why do you need to know?" Mrs. Burke asked her son. "You're not going to do anything stupid, are you? You can't leave the area by yourselves. It's much too dangerous."

"Mom!" said Steve.

"This is serious," said his father. "Your parents would be really angry, Alex, if I gave you information and then something happened to you. And you," he continued, turning to his son, "do not leave home. These are dangerous times. And I know what you're like," he added. "You do things without thinking."

"But Mr. Burke, I just want to try and get a message to Suze," said Alex.

"Won't you help us, Dad?" asked Steve.

"I'm sorry," said his father. "I know this is hard, but we just have to live with it. I don't want you or Alex rushing off. It's too dangerous out there."

The boys looked at each other. It was clear that they were not going to get any help from their parents.

As they climbed the stairs to his room, Steve asked his best friend, "Are you going to rescue your girlfriend?"

"Yes," said Alex. "I know my parents don't want me to try, but I have to. I don't care what anyone says, I have to rescue Suze."

Chapter 4

"It's not your job to think."

27.8.2110. 07.30.

A week had passed since Vic joined the police. Now, as he got ready for work, he thought about all the things he had learned in the past seven days.

He had learned that women stopped screaming if you fired your gun over their heads. He had learned that if you hit men in the knees, they fell down quickly. He had learned that most people were frightened of the police. He had learned that policemen worked in small groups, and that all the men in the groups were like brothers. He had learned that you did what your brothers told you to do. He had learned that the group was a family. He had learned that he belonged to the group.

There were eight men in his group. Some of them had been policemen for over fifteen years, but others, like Vic, were new. There was Matt, for example. Matt had been a policeman for a year, and he was two years older than Vic, but he already knew everything. Vic followed everything that Matt did.

"You see, Vic," said Matt, "here in the police, you belong to your group. This is your family. And your group protects you and you protect everyone in your group."

Vic nodded. He wanted to feel part of the group. He wanted to belong. He and Matt were sitting in the staff restaurant. The police got some of the best food in

London. They had their own farm and there was always plenty to eat. At the moment, they were eating eggs on toast. It was breakfast time and they were waiting for instructions.

"Now," said Matt, who felt that it was his duty to teach the new boy, "about this new Control Order . . ."

"Yes," answered Vic, listening to Matt and wanting to know more. "The new Order . . ."

"Now, you see, some people don't want to go to the camps," continued Matt. "That's understandable. They don't want to leave Britain. But then these people aren't British."

"No," agreed Vic. "They're foreign. But foreign wasn't always bad, was it, Matt? People used to travel in the old days. People came here and stayed. British people went abroad."

"That was the old days," replied Matt. "That was before the war. I wasn't alive then."

"Yeah," agreed Vic, eating his toast, thoughtfully. "My gran went to Spain once, I think."

"Yeah," said Matt. "You see, it was your grandmother. The world has changed. There was a European Union then. My dad knows all about the Union."

"My dad remembers it, too," said Vic. "One Europe and Britain at the heart of Europe. It sounds good."

"It didn't last after the war, though, did it? Since then, it's been every country looking after itself. There are strong countries and weak countries. Britain is strong. It's our tradition. That's why we wear a lion on our uniforms. Everyone knows the lion is the king of the animals."

Vic was only half-listening. He was thinking about all the things his father had said about the old Europe. "Wasn't there a tunnel from England to Europe?" he asked.

"What are you talking about?" Matt wasn't pleased. He didn't like it when Vic knew more things than him. Everyone had his or her place in the police force and Vic's place, as the new boy, was at the bottom. His job was to listen. Matt's job was to tell Vic about things. That was the way it was.

"A tunnel," Matt laughed. "Tunnels are for rats and terrorists."

"I thought . . ." began Vic.

"It's not your job to think, Vic. It's your job to do. Listen to me and do what I do. Right?"

"Right, Matt."

"And what's our job, Vic?"

"Our job is to get the foreigners to the camps, Matt."

"Exactly," continued Matt. "We don't want foreigners in Britain. We don't have enough food or water for foreigners. So we put them in the camps and then send them home."

"Right," said Vic again. There were three camps spread across Britain: Tilbury, Birmingham, and Buxton. All foreigners from London and the south of England were being taken to Tilbury.

Matt's phone rang. He picked it up and listened. "Breakfast is finished," he said. "We've got a job. A house in the Northeast district."

◇◇◇

Matt and Vic reached the house in thirty minutes. You could see that many years ago this was a beautiful house, thought Vic. It had big windows, and the rooms were each as big as his parents' old flat. This part of London was once the home of rich people. The houses were big and had gardens around them. Now, many of them had burned down. But people were still living in this house. An old man opened the door to the young policemen.

"What do you want?" he asked.

"Are you Mr. Palmer?" asked Matt.

"I am," said the old man.

"Then you know why we are here," said Matt.

"My wife and I have lived here for over fifty years," said the old man. "I was born in this house."

"And you can die in this house," laughed Matt. "We don't want you, you old fool. We've come to get Mrs. Palmer."

"My wife and I have been together for over fifty years," said Mr. Palmer again. "We have seen wars and floods, but we have survived. We have survived together. If you take my wife, then you have to take me, too."

"It doesn't work like that, Mr. Palmer," said Matt. "You are British. You stay here. Your wife comes with us."

"Please," begged the old man. "My wife and I are old. We've been together for fifty years. Please don't separate us."

"Your wife is Mrs. Palmer?" asked Matt. He looked at his list of names. "It says here that she was born in France."

"Yes," said the old man. It was hard for him. All of this was hard for him. "But she came to this country as a child." Mr. Palmer's voice shook. "She has lived in this country for over sixty years."

"Then this country has been good to her," laughed Matt. "But now it has to stop."

He and Vic went inside. The first things Vic noticed were the carpets on the floor. He had never seen a house with carpets before. But this house was on top of a hill. It had never been flooded. Vic liked the colors of the carpets. They filled the house with color.

Belle Palmer was sitting at the kitchen table waiting for them. The room was full of old things. The wooden table and chairs were like something Vic had seen in books. But everything was spotlessly clean; it was a beautiful home. Mrs. Palmer smiled at the young policemen. There was something about her that reminded Vic of his mother. Vic did not want to think about his mother at a time like this.

"Right," said Matt. "You're going to Tilbury Camp. Foreigners like you don't belong here."

He took the old woman by the arm; she smiled at him sadly, but did not resist.

Mr. Palmer stepped forward and tried to stop the young policeman, but Matt pushed him aside. He watched Matt take his wife through the door and it was clear, thought Vic, that he would have done anything to stop her.

"Belle . . ." Mr. Palmer muttered. He tried to reach her, but Vic pushed him back into the room. He fell down instantly. *Like the wall of a burned house*, thought Vic. *You just touch it and it falls.*

Matt took Mrs. Palmer out to the police van and put her in the back. The old man was on his knees, crying.

"Belle!" he called out. "Belle!"

Belle Palmer made no sound, but tears ran down her face.

Matt laughed briefly, but Vic suddenly found that he was being violently sick onto an old rose bush in the front garden. "That egg at breakfast was bad," he said to Matt as they drove away.

Chapter 5

Leaving London

3.9.2110. 06.00.

A summer fog, which began at sea, edged its way along the River Thames. At six in the morning, London was cool and it was still hard to see more than a few meters ahead. In their separate homes, Alex and Steve got up quietly, left notes on the kitchen tables for their parents, and then left.

"I've got to go and find Suze," Alex wrote. "Please don't worry about me." "We know where Suze is," wrote Steve. "And I'm going with Alex. I have to. I'm sorry, Mom and Dad."

They met each other at the gate that led to the street outside. The guards who protected the community were having their breakfast inside the guardhouse and nobody saw them leave.

The boys had decided that they would both go together to find Suze, though Steve had to work hard at first to persuade Alex that it would be good if he, Steve, came along.

"You don't have to come, Steve," Alex had said several times. "It's going to be very dangerous. Suze is my girlfriend."

"Stop being stupid, Alex," replied Steve. "If you're going, I'm going. I'm your best friend. You're going to need me."

The truth was that Alex actually wanted Steve with him very much. He was scared at the idea of crossing London and finding the camp. But he did not want to be responsible for something bad happening to his friend.

"It's my choice," said Steve. "You're not responsible for me. I'm going with you and that's that."

The two boys had talked and planned a great deal in the days since Alex found out that Suze was being held under Control Order 351. Alex felt like he'd aged thirty years in just a few days. It seemed a very long time since he'd been in the kitchen with his mother and Tish, talking about his birthday party.

The first thing he'd needed to do was find out where the police had taken Suze. But this had turned out to be easier than he had expected. Though the neighborhood guards were not the friendliest people, they had been more than willing to talk about the government's latest Control Order.

Alex had pretended to share their enthusiasm for Control Order 351. When he eventually asked where the foreigners were being taken, the guards told him: Tilbury Camp.

Now, as the two boys set out into the cold morning, Alex was glad to have Steve walking beside him. "We start walking east," he said, looking at the rising sun that was trying to break through the fog. "But we've got a long way to go. What do you know about Tilbury, Steve?"

"The Romans were at Tilbury hundreds of years ago," said Steve, trying to sound cheerful.

"That's not helpful, you idiot!" said Alex, smiling. "What else do you know?"

"Queen Elizabeth the First went there and spoke to her soldiers."

"Steve! That was over five hundred years ago. It's not going to help us now, is it?"

"You asked me what I knew," said Steve. "That's all I know. Anyway, you're the one who's been studying that old book of maps we found in your house. What do you know?"

"A lot more than you, it seems," said Alex. "Tilbury is a port. It's on the Thames where the Thames stops being the sea and becomes a river. And it's over forty kilometers from us here in London."

"Forty kilometers! Can we walk forty kilometers in a day?" asked his friend.

"I don't know," said Alex. "I've never tried to walk that far. Maybe we can do it in a day and a night. Or in two days. It's a long way. And we don't know what's between us and Tilbury. The map says the area is surrounded by wetlands that are extremely difficult to cross. There's also going to be Outsiders and fighting and we have to keep away from police and soldiers."

"Well, it's a good thing you've got me to keep you company on this adventure," said Steve.

"Steve," said Alex, suddenly turning serious. "I don't think this is an adventure. This is real life. And I'm only just starting to live it."

The words kept coming out. "I've been doing a lot of thinking over the last few days. It's like this is a war. Not a war like the Great War that destroyed most of the world. A war between what is right and what is wrong."

"Why should the government be allowed to control the lives of ordinary people? It's wrong to divide families and lock people up for no reason at all. The government says it's to keep us safe, but I don't feel safer with a government that's willing to force Suze and thousands of people like her to leave Britain. Do you?" Alex asked almost fiercely.

For a moment, Steve seemed speechless. Then he said: "You're completely right, Alex. It is a war. And we're finally joining the fight!"

Around them, the fog still moved around in damp clouds, giving them precious cover from suspicious eyes.

Chapter 6

Solo

3.9.2110. 06.00.

The young woman watched the fog as it covered the wetlands. Soon everything became gray and even the small trees and bushes were invisible. It was madness to try and cross the wetlands on a morning like this, but the young woman was not crazy. This was her home; she knew every centimeter of the land here and she knew the paths without needing to see them. She had crossed the wetlands in the dark since she was a child and she always felt safe here. Indeed, she felt safest on days like this when she knew that no one else was going to be there.

She liked being alone—she always had liked it. Solo, her mother called her, and it had become her name: Solo, a girl who did things quietly on her own. Solo had friends; there were many people who trusted her, but none of them knew her well. Nobody knew her history or where she lived. She was like a wild fox that comes into the city when it needs food, but then quietly disappears again.

Today she had to go into the city because the Farm needed a new piece of machinery. There were so many things that they could grow or find locally at the Farm. All the vehicles ran on oil from plants they grew, but when the trucks broke down, you had to know people who had access to the machine supplies. You needed a contact, a supplier. Solo had many contacts in London; she knew all the suppliers.

People trusted Solo. But she hated going into the city, because you never knew what was going to happen. It was dangerous.

Solo walked through the silent wetlands and hoped that her trip would be quick and without incident.

◇◇◇

It took Alex and Steve three hours to reach Woodford. They had kept away from the East Road, the one main avenue that connected London with the East Coast and all the major supply centers that were housed along the Thames.

"Where are we?" asked Steve.

"You asked me that fifteen minutes ago," said Alex. "We're in the wood that leads to South Woodford. We're getting close to the wetlands."

"I've never been in a wood before," said Steve. "It's really dark."

"That's because of the trees," said Alex.

Suddenly, through the trees, they heard a sound—a sound of fear and anger, halfway between a scream and a shout.

"What's that?" said Alex, but Steve was already running.

"Where are you going?" shouted Alex, running after him. "This isn't school, it's dangerous!"

There was a space inside the wood where there had been trees, but someone had cut them down. There, Alex and Steve saw a young boy and two men. The men were hitting the boy, who was on his hands and knees trying to get away from them.

"Stop that!" shouted Steve, running toward them.

"Watch out!" cried the boy. "He's got a gun!"

Steve continued to run toward the men, and one of them moved away from the boy and pointed the gun at Steve.

Moving without thinking, Steve threw himself at the man and knocked the gun from his hand. The gun fell to the ground, and the boy quickly picked it up.

The whole thing happened very suddenly. The second man looked at Alex and Steve, and then at the boy who was now holding the gun. He decided that it would not be wise to fight them, and hurriedly ran off into the dark shadows of the wood. The first man got up and made the same decision. Holding his arm in pain, he followed after the second man.

The young boy swung the gun round and pointed it at Alex and Steve. "What are you doing here and what do you want?" he demanded.

"Whoa!" shouted Alex in alarm. "What are you doing? We just rescued you! We don't mean any harm."

"Sorry," the boy replied, still keeping the gun aimed at them. "These are dangerous days. I'm just being careful. You are total strangers."

"We're trying to get to Tilbury Camp. Alex is trying to rescue his girlfriend. She's been taken there by the police under Control Order 351," said Steve.

The boy narrowed his eyes and looked at Alex, then Steve. Both of them hardly dared to breathe under that intense gaze. Suddenly, the boy lowered the gun and held out his hand with a smile.

"I believe you," he said. "Thanks for coming to my rescue. It was kind of you to help. My name's Solo."

Steve and Alex looked at Solo and realized that the boy they had rescued was, in fact, a girl.

"We're glad we could help you. I'm Alex and this is Steve," said Alex, as Solo shook his hand, and then Steve's.

"There's not much you can do against a gun," said Solo, "but I didn't have one with me today. This used to be a safe path. I didn't expect to run into those thugs."

"Are you okay?" asked Alex.

"Yes," said Solo. "A few bruises, but no major damage. Thanks to you," she added.

But Steve couldn't reply, because his mouth had suddenly gone dry. He had just realized that he'd run straight toward a man with a gun. If the man had fired the gun, he would be dead now. Steve leaned heavily against a tree, before sliding to the ground and sitting there in shock. Solo looked at him curiously.

"You haven't done much real fighting, have you?" she asked.

"No," said Alex. "That was our first real fight."

"Well," said Solo. "If you're going to walk around East London, it's not going to be your last."

Alex and Steve stared at her. They began to understand the world they were now in. And it was frightening.

"Why were they attacking you?" asked Alex.

"They wanted some information about the Farm," said Solo. "I didn't want to tell them."

Alex looked at her amazed. She was so young and so brave.

"But we can't stay here now," Solo went on. "Those thugs may have friends near here. We don't want to meet a group of them. My van is only five minutes away. You can come with me."

"Thank you," Steve managed to say.

"You're welcome," said Solo. She looked again at Alex and Steve, and laughed. "Two rich boys alone in a dirty little wood in East London. You're just babies in a wood full of hungry wolves." She shook her head in admiration.

We're not rich, Alex was about to say. But then he thought about the London that was all around him. This part of London was nothing but ruins and destruction. Compared with this, he and Steve were rich. Their world was a safe and clean world, inside a dark and dangerous one.

"So. How are you going to get to Tilbury?" asked Solo. "There are watchers on the roads and the police are traveling to and from the camp day and night."

"We thought we would try and get through the wetlands," said Alex.

Solo laughed. "You wouldn't last ten meters in there," she said.

"How do you know?" asked Alex.

"Because I've lived there all my life," she replied.

"That's wonderful. Then you can show us the way," said Steve.

"Well," said Solo, hesitating. "It's true that you did just save my life." She looked at the two boys again. It was clear that they knew nothing of her world. She guessed that they lived in some guarded community in the center of London, a place that was very different from the wetlands.

"OK, I think I can help you," she said. "But now let's move before they bring back some friends."

"Where are we going?" asked Alex.

"I'm taking you to the Farm," she said. "It's on the edge of the wetlands in Orsett. The group I work with live there."

"Are they Outsiders?" asked Alex.

"Yes," laughed Solo. "We're all Outsiders. We grow vegetables at the Farm," she added. "Actually we supply Tilbury Camp with vegetables."

"So you go right inside the camp?" asked Steve excitedly.

"Yes," said Solo.

"Then you can help me find my girlfriend!" said Alex.

Solo gave him an understanding smile. "Do you have any idea how big the camp is?" she asked. "Yes, I go into the kitchen with vegetables, but I don't see the prisoners. They live in low gray buildings and there are dozens of these buildings. You could spend days looking for your girlfriend. The camp is like a small city. And unless you have a map of the city you will just get lost."

"Then we'll just have to figure something out," said Steve, smiling at her.

Chapter 7

"I don't belong here."

3.9.2110. 07.00.

Vic sat on his bed looking out at the foggy street. It was going to be a difficult day if the fog did not clear. The drive to Tilbury was hard enough, because it was not easy to find the right streets when so many houses had been burned down and the street signs removed. The thick fog would make it twice as hard. Plus, Vic disliked the thought of driving through Barking in the fog; he would not be able to see who was coming. There was a group of Outsiders in Barking who had shot at the van twice in the past week. Driving to and from the camp was getting more and more dangerous.

But it was not the fog that was really worrying Vic. It was something much worse than the weather. It was the realization that he was not enjoying being a policeman at all. Not one bit. He'd pushed the thought away at first, because he had worked and wanted so long to be a policeman. But whenever he looked at all the other men in his group, he knew in his heart that he did not belong with them.

Every day they picked up more and more foreigners and took them to the camp at Tilbury. The sound of crying haunted him day and night. And he kept thinking about Mr. and Mrs. Palmer. He had met many other old people like the Palmers and had taken them away, but there was something about the Palmers that had stayed with him.

I don't like this job, he said to himself. *I don't like what we are doing to innocent people.* Vic sighed. It was never a good idea to think about these things. It was better to just do them, as Matt was always telling him. Anyway, he could never let his parents go back to their old home; they were so happy here.

Actually—Vic interrupted his own train of thought—it was his father who was really happy. His mother had recently started to look tired and worried again. Vic wondered whether she was ill. He went to the kitchen where his mother was washing up the breakfast dishes.

Vic paused a moment to watch his mother as she carefully put the plates away. But before he could speak, his mother said in a low voice, "Vic dear, there's something I need to tell you."

"Sure, Mom," said Vic in mild surprise. He needed to be at work in a few minutes, but he knew that Matt would ring if there was an urgent job.

"You know about these foreigners . . . ?" Mrs. Hall began.

"The ones I have to take to the camps?" Vic nodded.

"Yes, those." She hesitated again. It seemed as though she was trying to decide not just what to say, but whether she should even continue. She picked up a cup from the table beside her and took a drink.

"Oh, it's cold. I hate cold tea," she said.

"I can make you some more," offered Vic.

"No, don't bother, Vic. I don't really want it," said his mother.

"What is it, Mom?" Vic asked her.

His mother looked at him. "Tell me, how do the police know that these people are foreign?"

This was the last question Vic expected his mother to ask. "Because their parents come from another country," he replied.

"Just their parents?" she asked.

"Yes," said Vic.

"You don't pick them up if one of their grandparents came from abroad?" Her voice was shaking slightly.

"No." Vic shook his head. "Well, not yet," he said. "I've heard some policemen saying that this situation could change. Maybe it will change after we've picked up everyone whose parents come from abroad. Then, if there are still problems with everyone having enough food, we could start looking at people's grandparents."

His mother went white. For a moment, she couldn't speak. Finally, she managed to whisper unsteadily, "Well, if that happens, son, then you're going to be picking me up."

Vic knocked against the table and the teacup fell over, spilling a small stream of tea.

"Oh dear," said his mother automatically. "I'll get a cloth."

"Forget the cloth!" Vic found he was shouting. "What do you mean I'd have to pick you up?"

"It was my grandmother. Your great-grandmother," said Mrs. Hall. "She died before I was born. But she came from Italy."

"Italy!" said Vic.

"Your dad doesn't know," said his mother. "He must never find out."

Vic looked at her in astonishment. "Why didn't you ever tell me?" he demanded.

"There was no need," said Mrs. Hall. "And you know your father. He lives in another world. His father was the same. They never accepted that the country had changed. Even before the war. Of course, after the war, there were so many people who thought the same way as your father. That was when the government first announced that 'Britain was for the British.'"

"I thought the war was bad," continued his mother. "But I think that this is worse. It turns friends against each other: people you've had tea with, people you've been at school with. Suddenly they're enemies. A long time ago Britain was a country that welcomed foreigners."

She picked up the teacup and looked at it. "So that's why I'm worried, son," she said. "If they start looking at the grandparents, they'll come for me. I've been thinking about it, Vic. I've been thinking about it a lot. If that happens, I'll go."

"Go where?" asked Vic.

"Outside. I'll have to become an Outsider."

"But it's dangerous Outside. There's nothing there. You wouldn't survive, Mom."

"I couldn't do it to you, son," his mother smiled at him. "You couldn't arrest your own mother. I'll just go away one day, quietly."

Vic looked at his mother. She looked the same as she always did, old and tired, with that half smile he loved so much. She looked at him and brushed his hair out of his eyes. It was something she always did. Vic hugged her tightly.

She was his mom and he loved her. If it was within his power, she was never, ever going to a camp to be sent away from Britain and her family.

Later that evening, Vic sat in the police club and watched the men drinking and laughing. He and Matt had had a fairly easy day. They had taken three people—a father and his two daughters—to Tilbury Camp in the van and although the fog had been bad, there had been no attacks. Though the two girls had been born in Britain, their father had come from Portugal over thirty years ago. His daughters had cried all the way to Tilbury, and even the loud music that Matt played did not block out the sound.

Vic watched Matt as he sat with other members of the group and laughed at some joke. The crying never bothered Matt; Vic suspected that he didn't really hear it. But Vic heard it all the time. *I don't belong here*, he said to himself. *I don't belong anywhere.*

Chapter 8

On the Outside

5.9.2110. 05.30.

"Hey Alex, are you awake?" Steve sat up in bed. It was their second night in the small hut, sleeping on a pile of rags and newspapers, and he was not enjoying it.

"I am now," replied Alex sleepily. "What is it?"

"I think there's something inside the hut," said his friend.

"It's probably a rat," said Alex. "Or a mouse. Or maybe it's a snake."

"Yuck," Steve put on his shoes and stood up. "Do they have snakes here?" he asked.

"I don't know," said Alex. "What's the time? It's still dark outside."

"It's half past five," said Solo from outside the hut. "We're leaving in ten minutes, so you boys need to hurry."

Suddenly, Alex was wide-awake. He did not want the truck to leave without him. Today he and Steve were going to the camp at Tilbury with the morning delivery of vegetables.

Everyone at home in London grew vegetables, but here in this strange place, surrounded by dangerous wetlands, there were huge fields of carrots, beans, and potatoes. Even chickens, cows, and sheep were kept for their eggs, milk, and wool. But the biggest surprise had been the people on the Farm. *They have been so kind to Steve and me,* thought Alex. He didn't know what he had expected, but it certainly wasn't this.

Perhaps it was the name, "Outsiders." When people talked about the "Outsiders," it was always about the fighting and destruction they caused. They were the people who carried guns and tried to blow up government buildings.

Yet the Outsiders on the Farm were not in the least dangerous or violent. They had their own world as farmers and the only thing they wanted was peace and quiet. On the Farm itself, they were safe, they said. The police never came there because they were afraid of the wetlands, but on the road it was different. They were always in danger.

Alex and Steve liked the Farm and the people there very much, but what they heard depressed them. Everyone said that it would be impossible for two teenage boys to rescue Suze from inside the detention camp.

"Why don't you both go to the camp with the vegetables tomorrow morning?" suggested one of the men. "Then you can see it for yourselves."

Alex and Steve were excited about going to the camp, but also disappointed that they were going to be so close to Suze and yet unable to rescue her. "We've come so far, yet we still haven't thought of a way to get Suze out of the camp," said Steve.

"Is the camp heavily protected?" asked Alex as Solo drove the truck down the smooth, straight road that led to the camp.

"Yes, very. There might not be a lot of guards on duty, but it's a high-security camp all the same. There are security cameras everywhere and an electric fence surrounding the camp. And it's all centrally controlled from the camp's Control Room," said Solo.

The truck was very old and it did not go very fast. It was because of this that the police van came up behind them so quickly.

Solo saw the van first. She swore.

"What is it?" asked Steve.

"It's the police," said Solo. "And they're right behind us. Quick, climb into the back and hide under the tarpaulin!"

◇◇◇

Vic and Matt had been up all night. They were both tired and annoyed that they had to drive out to the camp after working for so many hours.

It was all because of a husband and wife who had tried to escape the police. The couple had left their home and had hidden in the basement of a ruined church. Vic and Matt spent most of the night talking to neighbors and informers before they found them. The man had come from Slovenia and now he was going to the camp. His British wife had been left behind, screaming, in the old church as Vic and Matt took her husband away.

At least the man was not making any sound, thought Vic. He looked around. It was dawn and the sky was just beginning to lighten. So far their van had not been attacked. But you could never be too sure.

They were about six kilometers from the camp when they saw the truck.

"I haven't seen a truck on this road before. What's it doing here?" Vic asked, more puzzled than suspicious.

"No idea," said Matt, speeding up. "But we can find out." He drove the police van in front of the truck and forced it to stop.

"Police!" shouted Matt. "I want to see your papers." He and Vic took out their guns and Matt walked to the driver's door.

"Get out of the vehicle!" Matt yelled into Solo's face.

"I'm just taking vegetables to the camp," said Solo, not moving. "I do it every day. Here, it says so in my papers."

Vic reached for her papers and quickly examined them. "Her papers seem to be perfectly in order, Matt," he said.

But Matt was in a bad mood and now he was looking for trouble. "She still hasn't obeyed me. Look at her, still sitting there. I think we should arrest her and take her back to headquarters for questioning. Maybe she knows something about those Outsiders who are attacking us," he snarled. "I'm going to search the truck!"

◇◇◇

Under the tarpaulin, Alex and Steve heard Matt's words in horror. But there was nothing they could do now. A moment later, Matt tore the tarpaulin from the truck with a sharp pull, revealing the two boys among the vegetables.

For Alex, the next few moments passed as if in a bad dream. He saw Matt's mouth open in an angry shout as he pulled his gun. On his right, Steve was already half-standing when Matt fired his gun. A look of shock flew across Steve's face, and then he fell back with his eyes open, not moving. Blood spread across his chest.

With a shout, Alex threw himself at Matt and took the gun away from him. He managed to throw Matt to the ground before backing away, breathing hard. There was an awful pause as Matt slowly stood up. Without warning, he charged at Alex with a look of pure anger in his eyes.

There was no time to think. Alex pulled the trigger on the gun. The sound of a gunshot rang out into the morning once more. By the time the sound had died away, Matt was lying on the ground, dead.

Alex, Solo, and Vic stood frozen in shock. Then Alex rushed to the side of his fallen friend. Holding Steve's body in his arms, he said, *"Why did he shoot him? We didn't even have a chance to explain."*

Meanwhile, Solo had picked up Matt's gun and was pointing it at Vic. "Don't move," she said fiercely, holding back her tears. "We've had enough killing for one day."

But Vic was still too shocked to move. He heard Solo's voice. It sounded like it was coming from far away, even though he could see her in front of him. The thoughts came into his brain: *Matt is dead. And before he died, he killed a boy.*

Matt is dead. And a boy, a teenager just like me, is dead too. Vic felt like he couldn't breathe. He felt like a great weight had settled on his chest, and was slowly taking his breath. He'd never seen anyone die. Now, in the space of just a few minutes, he'd seen two deaths. Two needless deaths. It wasn't right.

Vic looked at Solo. He knew she was an Outsider, but he felt a great longing to be like her. He no longer believed in being a policeman. He no longer believed in the government, or in Control Orders. They were the things that had led to this tragedy.

Solo's voice interrupted his thoughts. "Take out your gun and throw it on the ground," she told him. "Do it!"

Vic almost felt glad as he threw his gun on the ground and kicked it angrily away. It was a symbol of all that was wrong with Britain.

Chapter 9

The plan

5.9.2110. 06.00.

The rays from the rising sun crept along the road. In the pale morning light, the sad little scene seemed even sadder. Alex wept quietly over Steve's body, while Vic stood silent and unmoving.

Solo wished she could give Alex time to mourn his friend, but she knew they could not stay here in the road. They would be in a lot of trouble if someone came along and discovered them.

"Alex," she whispered urgently, "we can't stay here. You have to get up. We have to move."

Alex looked up at Solo with reddened eyes and nodded.

"Here, take this gun." Solo gave Vic's gun to Alex. "I need you to look after the policeman. Hide yourselves and the van in that little wooded area about three kilometers back. I have to deliver the vegetables to Tilbury Camp, or there will be trouble. I'll come back and find you."

She pulled Alex to his feet and touched him gently on the shoulder. Then she got into the truck and drove off. Alex drew a deep breath and walked over to Vic.

"I'm sorry about your friend," Vic said.

Alex looked into Vic's eyes and saw only sorrow and

sincerity there. But he didn't feel ready to forgive the young policeman yet.

"Help me get my friend and yours into the van," Alex said shortly. "We can't leave them here. You have to come with me too until Solo and I decide what to do with you."

Vic bit his lip. He understood how Alex was feeling and could not blame him for his harsh words. Wordlessly, he walked over to Matt's limp body and began to lift it into the van. Alex watched him for a brief moment. Then he went over to help.

Alex and Vic moved quickly, and had soon driven the van to the little wood where Solo had told Alex to wait. There was an awkward silence as Alex and Vic waited in the police van. Alex kept looking over at Vic, keeping his gun trained on him all the while.

"I'm sorry about your friend too," Alex finally said to Vic. "It was all a horrible accident. But he didn't need to shoot Steve. We hadn't done anything wrong. He didn't even give us a chance to explain."

Vic nodded slowly. "I don't blame you. Matt shouldn't have done that. He had a bad temper and it made him do stupid things sometimes. Now it's got him killed.

"Still, Matt was my friend. And now he's gone. It's just so stupid. Neither of them had to die. You say you're sorry. I'm sorry too."

Alex had not spoken to a policeman before, but he was pretty sure they didn't say things like that. He frowned, "You know, you don't sound like a policeman . . ."

Vic smiled—a very small smile. "Strange that you should say that," he said. "I've been wondering lately whether I really want to be a policeman. Nothing about this job makes me feel good." He paused reflectively. "I thought I'd be helping to protect people, but instead I'm just bringing them pain and hurt. Separating people from their families and friends. All because of a stupid Control Order from the government."

Solo's head suddenly appeared at the window. "It sounds like you don't want to be a policeman anymore," she observed.

"Solo!" Alex cried.

"I've delivered the vegetables, and the truck is parked just over there. Now I think we should all go back to the Farm so we can decide what to do next."

"The Farm?" asked Vic.

"It's where a group of us Outsiders live," said Solo. "We grow vegetables and raise animals. We don't rely on the government, and we don't live under the government's control."

Solo was watching Vic closely. "I think we can trust you not to betray us, but I want to be sure. If you go to the Farm with us, you won't be able to go back home afterwards. Do you understand what I'm saying?"

"Yes," Vic replied. "I have to make a choice. I don't fully understand any of this yet, but I know I can't go back to being a policeman. It's not just the shooting. It's everything."

"All right then," Solo nodded. "I hope I'm right in trusting you."

"By the way," said Alex, "I'm Alex, and this is Solo." He held out his hand.

Vic knew this was Alex's way of saying he did not blame him for what Matt had done. He took Alex's hand.

"I'm Vic."

◇◇◇

Back at the Farm, a group of Outsiders was having a meeting with the headman of the Farm. Solo parked the truck and jumped out. "Some of the Outsiders from Barking are here," she said in surprise.

"Who are the Outsiders from Barking?" Alex asked.

"They're not exactly like us here at the Farm," Solo told him. "The Barking Outsiders believe in actively resisting the government. They do things like try to steal government data, and carry out attacks on government offices. Since Control Order 351 was announced, they have been targeting the police vans that transport people to Tilbury Camp."

The headman had seen Solo and Alex, and he called them over. Vic followed them uncertainly. He wished that he were not wearing his police uniform. People were staring at him, which made him uncomfortable. True, he was with Alex and Solo, but he was not at all sure that he would be welcomed on the Farm.

"What is he doing here?" the headman demanded of Alex and Solo. The Barking Outsiders remained silent, but they gazed at Vic with suspicion. They looked very different from the Outsiders on the Farm. The men were unshaven; the women had dirty-looking hair. All of them had deep shadows under their eyes. Every single one of them carried a gun.

"Mr. Lee," Solo began, "it's all right. This is Vic. He doesn't want to be a policeman any more. He wants to be one of us." She briefly told him what had happened that morning.

Mr. Lee was a tall, distinguished man and he listened to Solo seriously and without interrupting. His eyes were very kind, despite his strict appearance. Vic liked him instantly.

"Very well, Vic," Mr. Lee said at last. "If what you say is true, then you have my sympathy. Many people here feel the way you do about the government. Perhaps here at the Farm, you will finally feel that you belong."

"Thank you, sir," Vic said.

"Alex," Mr. Lee continued, "I'm very sorry to hear about Steve's death. He was a brave young man, and it was obvious that he was a very good friend to you.

"I called you and Solo over because I thought the two of you might be interested in what our comrades from Barking have to say." He gestured to a thin, dark-haired woman who was standing next to him.

The woman came forward and began to speak. "My name is Angela. We're from Barking, as you can see, and since the announcement of Control Order 351, we've been trying to disrupt the transportation of our fellow citizens, the government's so-called 'foreigners,' to Tilbury Camp.

"But our attacks on the road to the camp are only a short-term measure. What we really want to do is damage the entire camp by destroying its Control Room. The camp's security system is operated entirely from the Control Room, so if we destroy it, the camp will become useless."

"However, for the attack to happen, a small team will need to get into the camp to find the Control Room and disable the security system first. This is where we are hoping that you, Solo, can help us. You deliver the vegetables every day. You could take some of us with you in the truck. What do you think?"

Solo looked thoughtful for a moment, then she frowned and slowly replied, "It's not that easy . . . If I were discovered with Barking Outsiders, we would all be shot. It wasn't so risky to take Alex and Steve. They're from London. If I had been discovered with them, we would have been thrown out of the camp, but at least we wouldn't have been shot."

Angela kicked the ground in frustration and disappointment at hearing Solo's answer. "I see . . ." she said. But before she could say anything further, Vic spoke up and surprised them all.

"I can take you to the camp," he said. "I'm dressed as a policeman and the police van is just there. No one will ask any questions if I take you to the camp. We'll just pretend that you're foreigners whom I've arrested."

There was a silence. Everyone was thinking it over. Vic could see Solo and Alex clearly approved of his idea. He wasn't so sure about the rest.

"That would be a good plan," Angela said doubtfully, "except for one thing. How do we know you won't betray us and tell the camp guards who we are? How do we know we can trust you with our lives?"

Vic had not expected this. "I don't know." he said hopelessly. "How can I prove to you that you will be safe with me? All I can give you is my word. I will not betray you. I promise."

"That's enough for me!" Alex said. He had not meant to speak so abruptly, but he was getting annoyed that these adults seemed to have so little faith in Vic. Turning to Vic he said, "I trust you, Vic. You can take me to Tilbury Camp. I want to rescue my girlfriend. And I want to help carry out the attack on the camp."

Angela looked at Alex and Vic. "Two young men with nothing to lose but their ideals, and maybe their lives," she said, "just like the rest of us.

"All right then." She turned to Vic. "Since Alex has put his trust in you, then we will trust you too. Anyway, I don't think we have a choice. There's no other way of getting into the camp."

Alex and Solo both smiled at Vic. He saw that they had complete confidence in him. It made him feel better than he had in a long time.

Chapter 10

Tilbury Camp

6.9.2110. 11.30.

The van drove over the road to Tilbury Camp. Vic, who was driving, could already see a distant line of buildings surrounded by an electric fence. Even in the late morning sunshine, the camp looked menacing.

"Look," Vic said over his shoulder. "There's Tilbury Camp." From the back of the van, Alex raised his head to take his first look at the detention camp. Beside him, Angela sat up, ready for action.

Next to Angela was another Barking Outsider named Jonathan. He too, looked up to see the approaching camp. But if he was nervous, he did not show it.

Angela raised her voice above the sound of the engine. "OK, guys," she said, "we're getting near the camp. Here's the plan, one last time."

"As we've agreed, we'll split up once we're inside. Alex will search for his girlfriend, Suze, while Jonathan and I try to find the camp's Control Room."

"Once Suze is found and we know where the Control Room is, we can begin the attack. Unfortunately, we won't know how to best disable the security system until we've seen how the Control Room is protected . . ."

The van suddenly went over a deep rut in the road, forcing everyone to grab their seats. Angela quickly steadied herself and continued, "A small army of Outsiders is going to hide out in the woods just outside the camp, ready to help us free the camp once the security system is down. With luck, we won't keep them waiting too long."

She took a deep breath. "Everyone ready? Once we pass through the camp gates, there'll be no turning back."

This is it, Alex thought. He felt the nervousness in his stomach. He'd barely been able to eat breakfast, and had slept badly. Thoughts of Suze, Steve, his family, and the camp had made him toss and turn throughout the night.

He wondered whether he would see his family again. *What if the plan failed? What if he or Angela and Jonathan were discovered? What if Suze had already been sent away? What if, what if, what if . . .* He'd been thinking all night about the what-ifs.

As they drew closer to the camp, Alex was determined not to let what-ifs stop him from rescuing Suze. He told himself there was no time for doubts; he just had to believe. The thought gave him strength, and as Vic drove the van through the great steel gateway of Tilbury Camp, Alex knew that he was ready for whatever came next.

Tilbury Camp was the size of a small city, and it was completely full of people. Yet, somehow, Alex had never felt so alone.

It had taken no more than half an hour for the efficient camp guards to register and process the three conspirators. A few papers to sign, a brief inspection of their belongings, and then Vic had driven away in his police van. Just like that, Alex and the two Barking Outsiders were prisoners at Tilbury Camp.

"Easy to get in, not so easy to get out," Jonathan had said as a guard led them through the camp. As Alex looked around him—taking in the security cameras and the electric fences—he silently agreed that the chances of escaping from the camp looked extremely small indeed.

It was a twenty-minute walk to the dormitory in Block D, Area 7, where they were to stay. The camp was filled with low-rise, gray concrete buildings. Each building was exactly like the others, and it would have been impossible to tell them apart if not for the block letter and area number painted on each building.

Even though children ran about playing games, the atmosphere in the camp was cheerless. Adults stood in small groups talking, or played board games, or simply slept. There was nothing else to do. Tilbury Camp was not exactly a prison, but it was definitely not a holiday resort either.

The guard took Alex and the two Barking Outsiders right to their beds. "Do what you're told," the guard warned them sharply, "and you'll be OK. But if you try to escape, or don't obey orders, you'll be shot." He turned and walked off.

Angela and Jonathan looked at the guard as he left. "I guess we should start trying to escape," Angela said. "See you later, Alex."

She and Jonathan immediately went into the camp to look for the Control Room, leaving Alex alone in the dormitory among the neat rows of camp beds. Sitting on his little camp bed with its uncomfortable woolen blanket, he wondered how on earth he was going to find Suze in the camp's vastness. He wished Steve was with him.

Come on, Alex! You're not going to find her by just sitting here, he scolded himself. He got to his feet and walked out of the dormitory to begin his search.

He walked and walked, and called Suze's name until he could hardly speak. But the camp was too big, and there were so many people in it. A hateful sense of defeat began to well up in his heart as he walked down yet another row of gray buildings. He rounded a corner and almost walked into two elderly women who were sitting together on a bench.

"Pardon me, ma'am," he asked the first of them, "have you seen a girl with light brown hair and brown eyes? Her name is Suze."

"Hundreds of girls like that here. Don't know what their names are," the woman answered. "Don't bother us, young man."

"Shh, Etta. He's only trying to find his friend," the second woman said. She looked at Alex. "Did you say your friend's name was Suze?"

"Yes," Alex replied. "She's my girlfriend actually."

"Well, in that case, you must certainly find her," the old lady's eyes twinkled at him. "I've met a Suze Stephens with brown hair and eyes; would that be your girlfriend?"

Alex's heart leapt. He couldn't believe his luck. "Yes!" he shouted. "Yes, that's her! Do you know where I can find her?"

The old woman's smile grew wider and kinder. "Suze is probably giving the children French lessons in Area 5. She's very good at French, your girlfriend."

"Yes, she's an A Plus at school and she taught herself to speak French." Alex hardly knew what he was saying; he was in such a fever to see Suze again. "Please excuse me, I must go and find her now. Thank you so much for your help!"

As he ran breathlessly in the direction of Area 5, Alex suddenly realized that he hadn't even asked the kind old lady her name. He'd been so excited to hear that she knew where Suze was. Feet flying over the ground toward Suze, he wondered if he would see the old lady again. He found himself eagerly hoping that the plan to free the camp would be successful, if only for the sake of people like her.

◇◇◇

Belle Palmer felt tears in her eyes as she watched the young man disappear into the distance. He reminded her so much of her husband, when he too had been a young man, and they had first fallen in love all those years ago.

◇◇◇

"Suze!" Alex shouted at the top of his voice.

"Suze, it's me, Alex! Where are you?"

His shouts rose into the air and echoed against the stone-gray buildings of Area 5. So far, he'd been answered only by silence and the curious stares of the people around him. He drew breath once more.

Suddenly, faint and far away, he heard her.

"Alex?" A figure emerged from the building's far end, and stepped out into the road.

But Alex knew her voice, and he was already running toward her. It was Suze! Her light brown hair shone as it caught the sunshine, like a spark of life in the middle of the camp's gloomy surroundings.

A moment later, he had folded her in his arms and was holding her tightly.

"What are you doing here?" Suze said breathlessly. "Oh, I'm so happy to see you, Alex. I've missed you so much."

"I'm glad to be holding you again too, Suze." He kissed her. For a little while they simply stood there with their arms around each other, relieved and thankful. It was Alex who was the first to remember where they were. Serious, he whispered, "Suze, there's a lot I have to tell you. Here, let's sit down."

Taking her by the hand, he led her to a nearby bench. Then, speaking softly in case someone could hear, he told her about the Farm, and the Barking Outsiders, and the plan to free the camp. Last of all, he told her about Steve.

Alex had thought he would never be rid of the ache that he felt in his chest whenever he thought of Steve. But as he told Suze about everything that had happened since he and Steve had left London, he felt the pain slowly begin to fade. Suze held his hand tightly and he knew she understood.

There was a brief pause full of silent memories. Suddenly, Suze frowned. "Did you say that the plan is to find the camp's Control Room and disable the security system?"

"Yes, because there are more Outsiders hiding in wait just outside the camp's fence. They'll help us subdue the guards and destroy the camp. But only once the electric fence is down. That's why Angela and Jonathan are looking for the Control Room right now."

"But Alex, I just realized I already know where it is!" The words came rushing out in her excitement. "It's hidden in plain sight. No one knows what it is because it's just another gray building like all the rest. But once, when I was playing with the children in Area 4, a government technician came to install a new security camera for the playground. After he fixed it up, I saw him enter this gray building nearby, and a moment later the camera made a beeping sound and started working. So you see, it must be the Control Room you're looking for!"

Alex smiled at his girlfriend. "Suze, you're brilliant! Come on, we've got to tell Angela and Jonathan. It's almost six-thirty anyway. Time we went to meet them."

Angela and Jonathan were already waiting outside the dormitory as Alex and Suze rushed up. From their expressions, Alex could tell that they hadn't found the Control Room.

"Good, you've found Suze," Angela said. "Jonathan and I haven't had any luck . . ."

"Angela, it's OK. Suze knows where the Control Room is!"

Angela's eyes widened, and even Jonathan looked impressed. "Really? You do? Where is it?" Angela turned to Suze, who repeated what she'd already told Alex about the technician and the security camera, and the gray building in Area 4 that looked like all the others.

"The problem is that we still don't know how to get in," Alex pointed out. "There's no electric fence . . . probably because they didn't want to draw attention to the building. Still, I'm sure there will be guards around."

But Angela just smiled at Alex. "Don't worry about it, Alex. Jonathan and I can handle it. We'll carry out the main attack on the Control Room. You and Suze stay in the camp. If Jonathan and I manage to disable the security system, then you two must tell everyone that an attempt is being made to free the camp."

She paused for a moment, then continued, "However, if Jonathan and I are killed—and there's always a chance that may happen—then I'm afraid you and Suze will have to figure out how to escape on your own."

Chapter 11

Rescue

7.9.2110. 21.00.

From the outside, nothing distinguished Block C, Area 4, from the rest of the buildings in the camp. It sat quietly on the far side of a playground, doors shut and windows closed, as if it was simply unoccupied.

However, Alex, Suze, and the two Barking Outsiders had spent the day observing the innocent-looking gray building and the guards who came and went from inside. What they saw confirmed their suspicions that Block C, Area 4, was almost definitely at the heart of the camp's security system.

"I can't think of any other reason why guards would regularly go in and out of an otherwise unoccupied building," Jonathan remarked. "So I'm pretty certain that it's the Control Room. The good thing is that there seem to be only two guards on duty at any time. That's going to make it a lot easier for us."

"Yes," agreed Angela, "I think we'll be able to do it. And once our support arrives, they'll help us defeat any remaining guards in the camp. In fact, I think we can begin the attack tonight."

Alex felt a thrill of fear and excitement. It was time!

◇◇◇

Looking round the edge of a building, Alex watched as Angela and Jonathan crept toward the entryway of Block C,

Area 4. The moon was high in the sky, and the buildings and trees made shadows over the ground. Even though Alex knew the two Barking Outsiders were there, he still struggled to keep sight of them as they disappeared easily among the shadows.

His heart thudded in his chest as he saw them again; they were almost at the door. The security camera above him made a sound as it moved round, before falling silent again.

This is crazy, Alex thought. *We're going to get caught and then shot.* The plan that had seemed so reasonable earlier now seemed the height of madness. With the Control Room right there and who knew how many guards around, it was impossible that they wouldn't be caught very soon. It was late, so they weren't even supposed to be out of their dormitories, let alone trying to get into the Control Room.

Suddenly, the sound of three sharp knocks broke the silence. It was Jonathan at the door. Then, springing back, he and Angela quickly hid themselves at the side of the doorway.

Time stood still. Slowly the door opened and a bar of light lengthened across the ground. In the doorway, Alex could see a guard holding a gun at the ready. The guard took a careful step forward, and then another.

But it was too late to avoid the punch that came at him from out of the darkness. Jonathan's punch hit the guard's jaw, throwing the guard backward through the open doorway. As his hands flew up in shock, Angela grabbed his gun and quickly turned to point it at him. However, the blow from Jonathan's fist had been a powerful one, and the guard was lying unconscious on the floor.

Alex realized he'd been holding his breath, and he let it out with a sharp gasp of relief. He watched as the two

Barking Outsiders pulled the unconscious guard into the entryway and shut the door. The moonlit scene became calm once more.

The attack had begun. Now it was up to him and Suze to alert the camp. Alex ran away to Suze's dormitory. There wasn't a moment to lose now.

He found Suze waiting just outside her dormitory. "How did it go?" she whispered anxiously. "Are Angela and Jonathan OK?"

"Yes, I saw them knock out one of the guards and enter the building. So far the plan is working. I think they'll be OK. We've got to do our part now and let people know there's a rescue operation going on. It'll be impossible to get everyone out of here if there's a panic."

"OK," Suze whispered. "But let's split up; we'll be faster that way. You alert Areas 1, 2, 3, and 4. I'll cover Areas 5, 6, 7, and 8. Be careful though. There are still some guards around."

"Yes, I know. You be careful too, Suze. I'll meet you back here soon, and we'll escape this camp together." He kissed her.

Moving silently from building to building, the two teenagers split up and walked across the camp, waking the other people in the camp to tell them about the rescue operation.

Alex was only halfway through Area 3 when all the lights went out, and the sound of an alarm wailed through the night. People started screaming. Alex had to shout to be heard over the noise.

"Everybody stay calm!" he shouted loudly. "We're trying to free the camp! Everybody please just stay calm and stay down!"

He hurried from building to building, trying vainly to control the growing panic.

Suddenly, a huge explosion lit up the sky, and Alex held back a cry of fear. It was impossible to tell whether the explosion had been set off by the Outsiders or by the government forces.

Alex no longer knew what was happening. The situation grew almost chaotic as one explosion after another went off in the distance. *Where are the other Outsiders?* Alex thought. *Surely they should be here by now!*

A jeep came tearing down the road with its headlights full on, heading straight for Alex. With its brakes making a terrible noise, it came to a stop just in time. With relief, Alex saw Vic and Solo jump from the jeep and run toward him.

"Solo! Vic! Thank goodness it's you! What's happening? Have we taken control of the camp?"

"The security system is down and we've destroyed part of the fence as well as the main gate. Those were the explosions you heard," Vic said.

"Yes," Solo continued, "and there are more explosives in the jeep to blow up the Control Room, but you have to show us where it is. Where are Angela and Jonathan?"

"I'm not sure. They'll probably be near the Control Room—that way. Come on, let's go!" Alex leapt into the jeep. The engine roared and the jeep sped off into the night.

Tilbury Camp was full of noise and movement. As the jeep went through the camp, Alex saw Outsiders fighting fiercely with camp guards, and other Outsiders who were busy organizing people into groups.

Then Block C, Area 4 came into sight. It was now completely dark and strangely quiet. As the jeep drew up, two shadows moved away from a wall and waved their arms. In the jeep's headlights, the shadows became Jonathan and Angela, who were keeping watch over two tied-up, unconscious guards.

Angela walked quickly over to the jeep. "Good. You've brought the explosives," was all she said. In the back of the jeep, Vic was already helping to unload the explosives.

By this time, Alex was starting to worry about Suze. "I've got to go and meet Suze," he said, "but I won't be long. The two of us will meet you back here, OK?"

"OK," Solo told him. "But make it quick. Once we've prepared the Control Room to explode, we're getting out of here!"

For the second time that night, Alex ran, heart beating loudly, toward Suze's dormitory. All around him, people were running in the opposite direction, led by Outsiders. As he moved past, Alex caught bits of what they were shouting.

"Everybody, please head toward the camp entrance!"

"Stay calm and everybody will get out all right!"

"We're taking you to a safe hiding place, and then you'll be able to go home to your families if you wish."

Men and women in the crowd were crying with relief as they joined the people moving toward the camp's entrance, which had now become its exit. A woman nearby hugged her children, crying, "Darlings, we're going home to Daddy!" as tears of joy rolled down her cheeks.

Suze was waiting for him outside her dormitory, and ran to meet him as soon as he appeared. Putting her hand in his with a smile, she said, "It's happening, isn't it, Alex? We're actually going to escape from the camp!"

"Yes! The plan is working! But we've got to hurry. They're waiting for us outside the Control Room," Alex said.

"OK then, let's go!" Suze cried. Hand in hand, they turned to run back toward the Control Room, leaving Suze's empty dormitory behind them.

The camp had emptied rapidly. A few Outsiders were checking the buildings for people left behind, and Alex could hear their shouts of "All clear!" ringing through the camp. Their work done, the remaining Outsiders got into waiting jeeps and sped toward the exit. One jeep pulled up next to Alex and Suze. The driver leaned out.

"Get in! We'll give you a ride out of here!"

"It's OK. We've got friends waiting for us!"
Alex shouted back.

"Alright," the driver nodded. "See you back at the Farm." With that, he drove off.

Solo already had the jeep's engine running when they rushed up to the Control Room. "There you are!" she shouted. "Come on! The explosives will be going off in a few more minutes!" The two Barking Outsiders were already sitting next to Solo in the front seat of the jeep.

Grabbing their hands, Vic pulled Alex and Suze into the back of the jeep. Solo started the engine and the jeep sped away. From the back of the jeep, Vic, Alex, and Suze looked back toward the dark Control Room and the empty camp buildings as they grew smaller and smaller. The explosives were timed to go off any minute now.

Alex's heart felt like it was in his throat. So much had happened, and it all seemed to come down to this moment. Tilbury Camp was going to be destroyed. *Steve, this is for you*, he thought.

With a great whoosh of sound and a blinding light, the Control Room exploded, throwing debris into the night sky. Solo, Vic, Alex, and Suze burst into happy cheers.

"We did it!"

Epilogue

13.9.2110. 10.00.

Vic stood outside a familiar house in Northeast London. The flowers in the large window looked like they needed watering, but otherwise the house on the hill looked exactly as it had before. Vic politely knocked on the front door.

Beside him, Belle Palmer stood holding his arm for support. Vic smiled down at her and laid his hand gently over hers. On the other side of the door, they could hear footsteps approaching. The door opened.

Mr. Palmer looked out, blinking like an owl.

"Belle?" His voice was filled with wonder. "Is that really you?"

With a wide smile, Belle Palmer held out her arms in reply. The old couple held each other for a long moment. Then turning to Vic, Mr. Palmer said slowly, "But I don't understand. You took Belle away. You and the other policeman. Are you going to take her away from me again?"

"No, sir. If it has anything to do with me, you and Mrs. Palmer will never be separated again. I'm sorry that it happened before."

Mr. Palmer looked carefully at the young policeman. "What happened? Why did you change your mind?"

"It wasn't so much a change of mind as a change of heart, Mr. Palmer. I've realized that I can no longer do as the government wants me to. So I've become a spy for the Outsiders."

"The Outsiders? I thought that lot are just dangerous thugs."

"Oh no, dear," Belle Palmer corrected her husband. "That's just what the government wants us to think."

"Mrs. Palmer is right," said Vic. "It was the Outsiders who freed the camp where Mrs. Palmer was taken. Tilbury Camp is completely destroyed now. However, I must warn you that Mrs. Palmer is still in danger if she stays in London."

Mr. Palmer looked alarmed. "But if they destroyed the camp . . . ?"

"Unfortunately, Mr. Palmer, arrests under Control Order 351 are still continuing. It's just that they're happening much more slowly because they need to transport the prisoners to the other camps in England."

Mr. Palmer looked so upset at hearing this that Vic hurriedly continued, "Many of the people who were rescued from Tilbury Camp have decided to join the Outsiders on their Farm. If you and Mrs. Palmer will quickly pack a few things, I can take both of you back to the Farm with me. You can live there in peace, until this government is finally overthrown and England is a free country."

"But are you sure Belle would be safe on the Farm?" Mr. Palmer asked. "How do you know the police won't raid the Farm and separate Belle and me again?"

"Mr. Palmer, I can't guarantee anything for sure. But I can say this: the Farm has been safe for twenty years now. You'll be safer there than anywhere else in England."

Mr. Palmer did not hesitate. "Alright. As long as Belle is safe and the two of us are together, that's all that matters.

If you can wait a few minutes, we'll put some things in a suitcase and come with you now!" he declared with a smile.

Vic returned his smile. "Of course I can wait. I was hoping so much you and Mrs. Palmer would come! I am at the Farm often, and it would be wonderful to see you when I visit." He nodded affectionately at the old couple.

Belle Palmer laughed. "Good, that's settled then!"

Vic laughed along with the old couple, feeling that he was now doing something that he knew in his heart was right. On the Farm with the Outsiders, he'd finally found a place where he belonged.

Review: Chapters 1–4

A. Match the characters in the story to their descriptions.

1. _____ Tish Davidson
2. _____ Mrs. Davidson
3. _____ Suze Stephens
4. _____ Steve Burke
5. _____ Vic Hall
6. _____ Matt
7. _____ Belle Palmer

a. Vic and Matt arrest this "foreigner."

b. Alex's girlfriend

c. Alex's mother

d. This young man has just joined the police.

e. Alex's sister

f. This person has been with the police for one year.

g. Alex's best friend

B. Choose the best answer for each question.

1. There are _____ Control Orders.

   a. 273

   b. 215

   c. 351

   d. 327

2. The British government considers a "foreigner" to be anyone who _____.

   a. has visited a country overseas

   b. has one parent who was not born in Britain

   c. speaks a language other than English

   d. has lived in Britain for less than twenty years

3. Vic worked hard to be a policeman because _____ .

　a. he wants to do what is right

　b. he likes the police uniform

　c. he wants to earn a lot of money

　d. he wants to make sure his parents are safe

4. In 2110, energy is generated by _____ .

　a. solar panels and wind turbines

　b. burning coal

　c. hydroelectric dams

　d. nuclear power stations

C. Read each statement and circle whether it is true (T) or false (F).

1. In 2110, there are only two television channels.   T / F

2. The Davidsons live comfortably compared to other Londoners.   T / F

3. Under Control Order 273, activities of more than twenty people   T / F
must be reported to the Control Room.

4. Steve Burke's parents think it would be too dangerous to try to   T / F
rescue Suze.

5. The European Union still exists in 2110.   T / F

6. "Foreigners" are being arrested because they are considered   T / F
Outsiders who live outside society.

7. Vic actually does not want to arrest Belle Palmer.   T / F

Review: Chapters 5–8

A. Complete the crossword puzzle using the clues below.

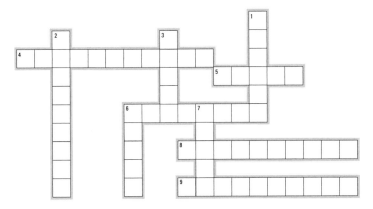

Across

4. Vic's mother is worried that she will soon be considered foreign because her _____ came from Italy.

5. Tilbury is over _____ kilometers from London.

6. The Outsiders on the Farm feel safe because the police are afraid of the _____ that surround the Farm.

8. The security system for Tilbury Camp is centrally controlled from the camp's _____. (two words)

9. The Outsiders on the Farm supply Tilbury Camp with _____.

Down

1. Alex finds out from the neighborhood _____ that arrested "foreigners" are being taken to Tilbury Camp.

2. Alex and Steve hide under a _____ when the truck is stopped by the police.

3. Steve is shot in the _____ by Matt.

6. For Vic, his gun has come to represent everything that is _____ with Britain.

7. Solo got her name because she likes being _____.

B. Number these events in the order that they happened (1–8).

a. Alex and Steve spend two nights on the Farm. _____

b. An angry Matt shoots Steve and kills him. _____

c. Alex and Steve set out from London on a foggy morning. __1__

d. Alex shoots Matt in self-defense. _____

e. Alex and Steve accompany Solo during the morning
delivery of vegetables to Tilbury Camp. _____

f. Alex and Steve meet Solo when they rescue her from
two attackers. _____

g. Matt and Vic stop the truck and ask Solo for her papers. _____

h. Solo tells Vic to give up his gun. _____

Review: Chapters 9–11 & Epilogue

A. Circle the best answer for each question.

1. The Outsiders choose to live on the Farm because _____.

   a. they like growing vegetables

   b. the government wants them to live far away from London

   c. they want to avoid living under the government's control

   d. they like the countryside

2. The Outsiders from Barking are different from the Outsiders on the Farm because _____.

   a. Barking Outsiders are committed to carrying out attacks on the government

   b. Barking Outsiders do not support the government

   c. Barking Outsiders do not respect Mr. Lee, the Farm's headman

   d. Barking Outsiders speak to each other in a coded language

3. Initially, Angela does not trust Vic to take them to Tilbury Camp. She thinks that _____.

   a. he looks untrustworthy

   b. he will crash the van and injure them

   c. he is a spy

   d. he will betray them to the camp guards

4. _____ tell(s) Alex where he can find Suze.

   a. A kind old man

   b. Belle Palmer

   c. A guard

   d. Angela and Jonathan

5. The Control Room in Tilbury Camp is protected by _____.

    a. being hidden in plain sight

    b. electric fences

    c. explosives

    d. camp guards

6. After the Control Room at Tilbury Camp is destroyed, _____.

    a. the prisoners are rescued and many become Outsiders on the Farm

    b. Belle Palmer is sent to another detention camp

    c. the government is overthrown and Britain becomes a free country

    d. arrests under Control Order 351 are stopped immediately

B. Complete each sentence using the correct word from the box. One word is extra.

Outsiders "foreigners" steel concrete explosives attack

1. Vic proposes to sneak the Outsiders into Tilbury Camp by pretending they are _____ whom he's arrested.

2. The camp is filled with low, gray buildings made of _____.

3. When the _____ begins, Alex initially does not know if the explosions are set off by Outsiders or government forces.

4. Angela and Solo set up _____ in the Control Room.

5. After Tilbury Camp is freed, Vic becomes a spy for the _____.

Answer Key

Chapters 1–4

A:
1. e; **2.** c; **3.** b; **4.** g; **5.** d; **6.** f; **7.** a

B:
1. c; **2.** b; **3.** d; **4.** a

C:
1. T; **2.** T; **3.** F; **4.** T; **5.** F; **6.** F; **7.** T

Chapters 5–8

A:
Across:
4. grandmother; **5.** forty; **6.** wetlands; **8.** Control Room; **9.** vegetables

Down:
1. guards; **2.** tarpaulin; **3.** chest; **6.** wrong; **7.** alone

B:
3, 6, 1, 7, 4, 2, 5, 8

Chapters 9–11 & Epilogue

A:
1. c; **2.** a; **3.** d; **4.** b; **5.** a; **6.** a

B:
1. "foreigners"; **2.** concrete; **3.** attack; **4.** explosives; **5.** Outsiders

Background Reading:

Spotlight on . . . *Dystopian futures*

BIG BROTHER IS WATCHING YOU

Writers of dystopian fiction take aspects of current society that are undesirable and develop them as the main theme of their stories. Often, they try to warn their readers about what our world could become in the future if we don't do something to change things while we still can. Control Order 351 belongs to this type of fiction. In this story, the author describes a futuristic fantasy world where the government controls every part of citizens' lives, both public and private. This results in a society where citizens find their freedoms restricted. An extreme case is the scenario where "foreigners" are deported to camps.

A recent example of dystopian fiction written for young adults is the 2008 novel *The Hunger Games*, which was later made into a movie. In this novel, Suzanne Collins wrote about the nation of Panem, which is politically controlled by a large and important city, called The Capitol. The story is written in the voice of sixteen-year-old Katniss Everdeen. She is forced to take part in an event called the Hunger Games. This is an annual contest in which participants are selected by lottery to take part in a televised "games to the death." This novel won praise for its storyline, and was one of *Publishers Weekly*'s "Best Books of the Year."

A very well-known example of dystopian fiction is the novel *1984*. Written by George Orwell and published in 1949, the novel is set in Oceania, a fictional society where people are controlled by a political organization called The Party. This political organization is led by a dictator called Big Brother. The government spies on its citizens and tries to control what they think. Individualism (that is, acting for yourself, not society) is discouraged and, in fact, punished. The main character in the novel is a man called Winston Smith, who works for the Ministry of Truth. His job is to rewrite old newspaper articles so that they support The Party.

Interesting, disturbing, and sometimes scary, dystopian stories make us think about the type of societies we would like to live in.

Think About It

1. Have you seen any movies or read any books about dystopian futures?
2. Do you think these types of dystopian futures could happen in your country?

Glossary

comrade   (*n.*)   a fellow soldier

conspirator   (*n.*)   someone who is planning something in secret

detention camp   (*n.*)   a camp where people are kept as prisoners

disable   (*v.*)   to put something out of action

dormitory   (*n.*)   in an institution, a large room where a number of people sleep

explosion   (*n.*)   a loud bang when a bomb or explosives go off

frown   (*v. & n.*)   a bad look; opposite of *smile*

jeep   (*n.*)   a vehicle often used for driving over rough land

natural resources   (*n.*)   supplies such as oil, coal, and wood

punch   (*v.*)   to hit someone with your fist

suspicious   (*adj.*)   doubtful or mistrusting

tarpaulin   (*n.*)   a cover usually made of canvas

totalitarian   (*adj.*)   a political system that has just one party, which controls everything

van   (*n.*)   a vehicle; a small truck often used for carrying things

wetlands   (*n.*)   land consisting of marshes or swamps

NOTES

NOTES

NOTES

NOTES